A HISTORY OF
VICTORIAN SKIRT GRIPS

A HISTORY OF VICTORIAN SKIRT GRIPS

MARY SAWDON

MIDSUMMER BOOKS
CAMBRIDGE

First published in Great Britain
in 1995
by Midsummer Books
an imprint of Silent Books Ltd, 10 Market Street,
Swavesey, Cambridge, CB4 5QG

© Text copyright Mary Sawdon 1995.

No part of this book may be reproduced in any
form or by any means without prior permission
in writing from the publisher

ISBN 1 85183 076 6

British Library Cataloguing-in-Publication Data.
A catalogue record for this book is available from the
British Library.

Typeset by GW Typesetting, Willingham Cambridge

Printed in Great Britain by St Edmundsbury Press, Bury St Edmunds, Suffolk

We are grateful to the following for permission to reproduce pictures:
The Gallery of English Costume, Platt Hall, Rusholme, Manchester;
The Glenbow Museum, 130-9th Avenue SE Calgary, Alberta, Canada;
The Ashmolean Museum, Oxford; York Castle Museum;
Wimbledon Lawn Tennis Museum Library; The Bettman Archive; Reed Consumer Books;
Norfolk Museums Service; Geffrey Museum; City of Nottingham Museum of Costumes
and Textiles; City of Bristol Museum and Art Gallery; Bath Museum Service;
The Public Record Office; Wygston's House Museum of Costume, Leicester;
Abington Museum, Northampton

CONTENTS

A history of Victorian skirt grips   7

Appendix   56

1 *A Young Englishwoman*, Hans Holbein II 1540

A HISTORY OF VICTORIAN SKIRT GRIPS

LITTLE has been written on the subject of skirt grips – their uses, users or inventors – despite their historical importance as a fashion accessory and today's intense interest in the development of women's clothing. Known variously as skirt grips, skirt lifters, skirt suspenders, porte-jupe and porte-robe, their popularity peaked during the nineteenth century, when metal craftsmen produced them in their thousands. However, ways of ensuring the length of the skirt were used well before – an appendage to the floor-length dresses worn from the sixteenth century. Indeed, the Ashmolean Museum, Oxford, has one of the earliest illustrations of a skirt suspender, in a water colour and pen and black ink drawing by Hans Holbein, dated 1540. This shows two clips on the ends of a waist girdle, which lifted the skirt well above the ground (Illustration 1). It is interesting to compare Holbein's suspender with that of another early example, said to be seventeenth century, at the Gallery of English Costume, Platt Hall, Manchester (Illustration 2). Thereafter, many elegant ways of lifting the skirt were used, notably where suspenders had cords with buttons, which were stitched and held in place discretely beneath the skirt.

The Victorian period was the golden age of the skirt grip. From the middle of the nineteenth century, as a score of entrepreneurs began to fight for their share of the market, extravagant skirt grips were designed, like the one dated as early as 1846 in C. Cunnington's book entitled *English Women's Clothing in the Nineteenth Century*:

> Dress clips called Pages formed in the shape of a negro's head, attached to the waist by a chain and used to clip and hold up the skirt when walking.

Similarly, in 1857, elaborate skirts are described as having pyramids of velvet or quiltings and the front 'en tablier', an appropriate setting for ornamental porte-jupe clasps. These were hung from the waist with a brooch attached to them, and this was – in turn – attached to two small rings sewn on the skirt.

In 1859, a new device, called the Watteau Porte-Jupe was introduced to render the skirt, in walking, more manageable. In this design, a ribbon covered the wire loop and a broad ribbon was attached, which hooked at the waist. A concealed buckle shortened the ribbon, and a fold of skirt was passed into the loop to save having to hold it up by hand. This fashion is described in detail in the *Englishwoman's Domestic Magazine* of January 1862:

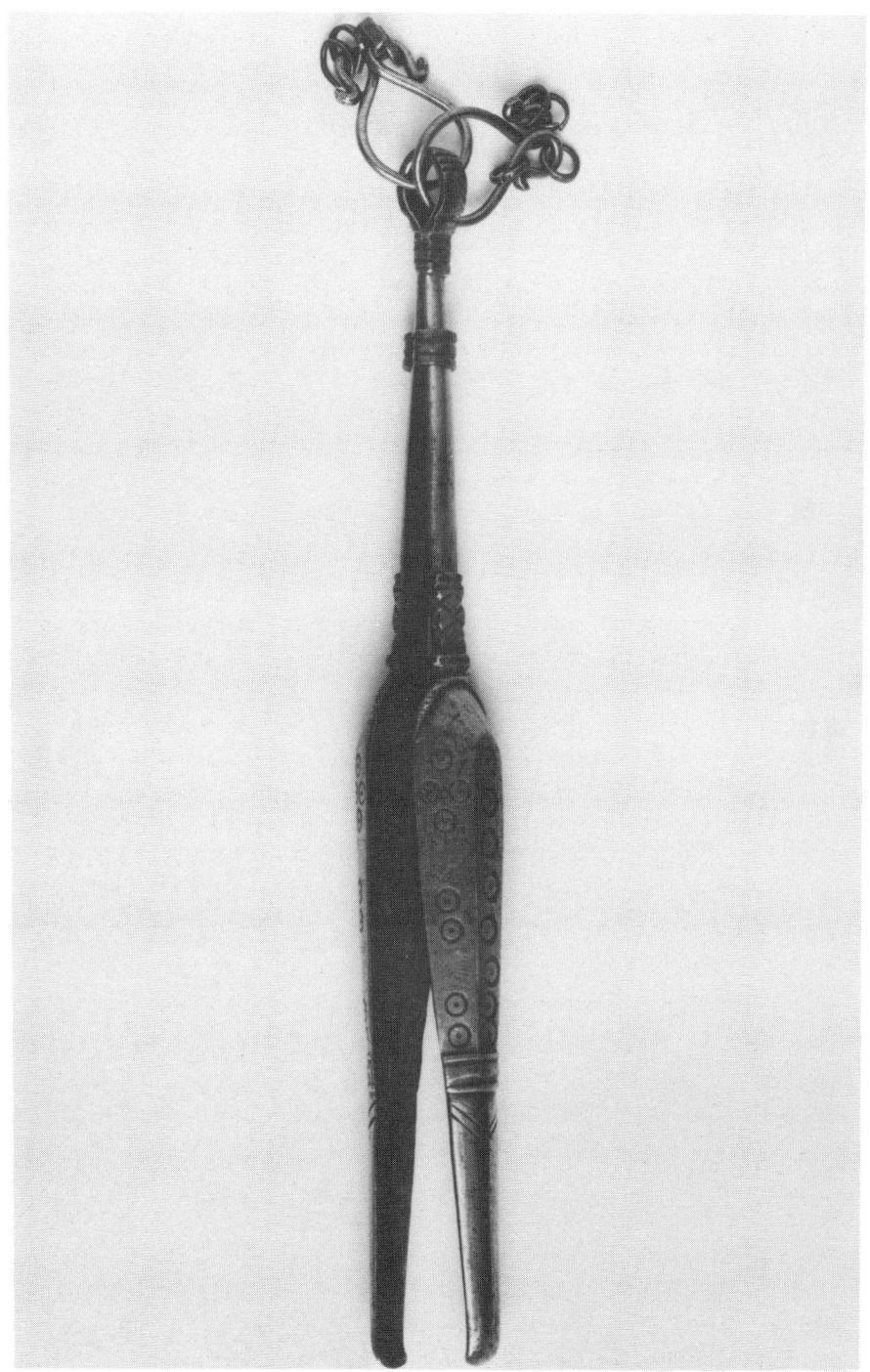

2 Skirt suspender c. seventeenth century

We all know the discomfort of having to hold up the dress in dirty weather, and the injury that a good silk dress sustains under the pressure of the hand. Petticoats are this winter made of such pretty designs, that dresses looped over these have really an elegant and graceful appearance. To obtain this result we can suggest three different modes of looping up dresses.

The first is by making a band to fit the waist, and attaching to this band six or seven ends of cord, with a loop made at each end. A button should then be sewn inside the dress, to the height of a quarter of a yard from the bottom, on every seam, and the loops of cord buttoned on the buttons. When this arrangement is complete, it has a very elegant appearance. Another style, which is frequently termed Le Watteau, is made in the same manner, with a waistband either of velvet or silk, and fastened by a clasp, or by bows or rosettes of ribbon. From this band a long loop is suspended on each side, the dress being drawn through the loops, forming festoons at the back and front. Another and very simple method is to have an elastic band fastened round the waist, and to pull the skirt through it all round the length required.

During the 1860s, French women's fashions emphasised the importance of the petticoat. Indeed, gowns were made with the skirt lifters already included in the make-up of the dresses, where the whole purpose was to raise the dresses as far as the ankle to show the colours and patterns of the petticoats beneath. In 1861, the English copied the French and there was a parallel rage for wearing long dresses which were also lifted to the ankle to flaunt elaborate petticoats made of cashmere, taffeta, rep or alpaca, perhaps embroidered or enriched with velvet. In a similar vein, the walking skirt, also caught up in order to reveal the petticoat, had two loops of elastic on each side on the inner surface, with a small slit through which they could be drawn out and looped on to buttons attached just below the waist. Here, two petticoats were worn, the first of cambric with a deep tuck, and the other of muslin with deep flounces. It was necessary when walking and when wearing these petticoats to use a porte-jupe.

The description in the Patent Book on 3 February 1858, of the first porte-jupe patent, which was made by W. E. Newton, is as follows:

> The cords pass over pulleys attached to the girdle worn under the dress, and all terminate in a knot, so that they can be drawn up by hand.

Other early patents followed, of course. The porte-robes or dress suspenders devised by Mr Benjamin Taylor and Mr Charles Edkins, both of Birmingham, indicate the slow and tortuous method of using them. These were patented in 1861 and were called 'Improvements in Porte-robes or Dress Suspenders, and also in Apparatus for the Suspension of Curtains, Draperies, and other Articles'. So, women had to have their wits about them or they might find they were hanging the curtains instead of hitching up their own skirt!

In the *English Woman's Magazine*, Volume 5, Number 1, under 'Supplemental

3   The 'Pompadour Porte-Jupe', the *Englishwoman's Domestic Magazine* 1862

Fashion and Needlework' (Price 6d), home-made designs were illustrated. Further, the *Englishwoman's Domestic Magazine* of May 1862 indicated how the skirt might be lifted up to show the wearer's attractive petticoat. The readers of this magazine appeared to have enough time not only to read about this device but also to make it, and it is worth considering the length of time needed to button all the buttons before stepping into the dress. All these methods could be made at home, reflecting the growth of home dressmaking that followed the invention of the sewing machine.

However, the expansion of domestic dressmaking was largely confined to the middle class: the rich continued to employ professional dressmakers and/or servants, and the poor passed down their clothes or wore them until they fell apart. Consequently, the *Englishwoman's Domestic Magazine* was written with middle-class women in mind and makes frequent reference to those active ladies who used dress suspenders when playing croquet, golf or tennis, or when dancing or even bicycling. Clearly, for this group, it was especially useful to have a convenient, easy-to-use skirt grip to keep the hem clean and off the ground.

A.D. 1865, 20th December. N° 3298.

Dress Holder.

LETTERS PATENT to Henry Edward Newton, of the Office for Patents, 66, Chancery Lane, in the County of Middlesex, Mechanical Draughtsman, for the Invention of "AN IMPROVED KIND OF CLASP OR DRESS PRESERVER TO PREVENT LADIES' DRESSES FROM TRAILING ALONG THE GROUND."—A communication from abroad by Marie Louise Changeur, of Boulevard Beaumarchais, Paris, in the Empire of France.

Sealed the 15th May 1866, and dated the 20th December 1865.

PROVISIONAL SPECIFICATION left by the said Henry Edward Newton at the Office of the Commissioners of Patents, with his Petition, on the 20th December 1865.

I, HENRY EDWARD NEWTON, of the Office for Patents, 66, Chancery
5 Lane, in the County of Middlesex, Mechanical Draughtsman, do hereby declare the nature of the said Invention for "AN IMPROVED KIND OF CLASP OR DRESS PRESERVER TO PREVENT LADIES' DRESSES FROM TRAILING ALONG THE GROUND," to be as follows:—

Various methods of holding up dresses have been employed, one of them
10 consisting of a nipper, between the jaws of which the material is held. This has been found very inconvenient, inasmuch as after a certain amount of use the nipper gets bent and the dress will slip away therefrom and fall on the ground. This system has given place to an arrangement of cords which will loop up the dress and will effect the intended object, but to the
15 detriment of the elegance of the dress.

Newton's Improved Dress Holder.

The object of this Invention is to construct and arrange a clasp in such a manner that it will answer the purpose, and yet not produce an inelegant effect.

The Invention consists in the employment of brooches, either straight or bent, arranged vertically or horizontally, and destined to unite in one or many points the several folds of the dress. A very important point is that the point of the pin of the brooch should be hidden to prevent it from catching and tearing any light material that may be employed. To effect this a small box is used, as in the case of the pins known as safety pins, instead of the ordinary catch. This brooch holds up the dress, and is attached by a chain or cord to another brooch or hook, which fastens it to the girdle or belt. Any number of brooches may be fastened round the girdle or belt, but two will generally be found sufficient. In cases where the material employed is likely to be injured by the pin of the brooch small rings can be placed at proper intervals round the dress. The lower brooch may be dispensed with, and small chains with hooks or brooches may be used instead.

It will now be understood that by raising the cord or chain to which the brooches or fasteners are attached and supporting it from the girdle, the dress may be looped up and prevented from trailing on the ground.

SPECIFICATION in pursuance of the conditions of the Letters Patent filed by the said Henry Edward Newton in the Great Seal Patent Office on the 20th June 1866.

TO ALL TO WHOM THESE PRESENTS SHALL COME, I, HENRY EDWARD NEWTON, of the Office for Patents, 66, Chancery Lane, in the County of Middlesex, Mechanical Draughtsman, send greeting.

WHEREAS Her most Excellent Majesty Queen Victoria, by Her Letters Patent, bearing date the Twentieth day of December, in the year of our Lord One thousand eight hundred and sixty-five, in the twenty-ninth year of Her reign, did, for Herself, Her heirs and successors, give and grant unto me, the said Henry Edward Newton, Her special licence that I, the said Henry Edward Newton, my executors, administrators, and assigns, or such others as I, the said Henry Edward Newton, my executors, administrators, and assigns, should at any time agree with, and no others, from time to time and at all times thereafter during the term therein expressed, should and lawfully might make, use, exercise, and

Newton's Improved Dress Holder.

vend, within the United Kingdom of Great Britain and Ireland, the Channel Islands, and Isle of Man, an Invention for "AN IMPROVED KIND OF CLASP OR DRESS PRESERVER TO PREVENT LADIES' DRESSES FROM TRAILING ALONG THE GROUND," a communication to him from abroad, upon the condition (amongst others) that I, the said Henry Edward Newton, my executors or administrators, by an instrument in writing under my, or their, or one of their hands and seals, should particularly describe and ascertain the nature of the said Invention, and in what manner the same was to be performed, and cause the same to be filed in the Great Seal Patent Office within six calendar months next and immediately after the date of the said Letters Patent.

NOW KNOW YE, that I, the said Henry Edward Newton, do hereby declare the nature of the said Invention, and in what manner the same is to be performed, to be particularly described and ascertained in and by the following statement, reference being had to the Drawing hereunto annexed and to the letters and figures marked thereon (that is to say) :—

All the arrangements that have been proposed hitherto for holding up ladies' dresses and preventing them from trailing in the mud or dust have more or less attained the desired result.

The arrangements which have hitherto been employed (one of which consists of a nipper, between the jaws of which the material is retained) have been found very inconvenient, inasmuch as after a certain time the jaws of the nipper become bent, and the dress will slip away therefrom and fall on the ground. This system has given place to an arrangement of cords which will loop up the dress, and will partially effect the desired object, but at the same time with detriment to the elegance of the dress.

The object of the present Invention is to attain all the desired results, and it consists in the employment of brooches, either straight or bent, arranged vertically or horizontally, and intended to unite in one or many points the several folds of the dress.

In the accompanying Drawings are shown several methods of attaining the desired result. A very important object is that the point of the pin should be hidden so as to prevent it from catching and tearing any light material that may be worn. To effect this a small box is used, as in the case of the "safety pins" instead of the ordinary catch. When the "safety pins" are used, the form is modified slightly as shown at A, Fig. 1. This brooch or safety pin holds up the dress and is attached by a chain or cord to another brooch or hook C, which fastens it to the girdle or belt. Any number of brooches may be fastened round the girdle or belt, but two will generally be found sufficient. In some cases, where the material employed is likely to be injured by the pin of the brooch small rings can be placed at proper intervals round the dress. The lower brooch may be dispensed with, and small chains with hooks may be used instead, as shewn at Fig. 4. In Figs. 3 and 4, the brooches are represented in an ornamental form, but this is not absolutely necessary. Fig. 5 represents the application of this system and the effect produced. It will be understood that by raising the cord or chain to which the brooches or fasteners are attached, and supporting it from the girdle, the dress will be looped up and prevented from trailing on the ground.

Having now described the nature of the said Invention as communicated to me by my foreign correspondent, and having explained the manner of carrying the same into effect, I wish it to be understood that I claim as the Invention secured to me by Letters Patent as aforesaid, the application of brooches in general for dress preservers, and their application to this purpose by means of the arrangements of parts herein shewn and described.

In witness whereof, I, the said Henry Edward Newton, have hereunto set my hand and seal, this Eighteenth day of June, in the year of our Lord One thousand eight hundred and sixty-six.

H. E. NEWTON. (L.S.)

Witness,
J. W. MOFFATT,
66, Chancery Lane.

LONDON:
Printed by GEORGE EDWARD EYRE and WILLIAM SPOTTISWOODE,
Printers to the Queen's most Excellent Majesty. 1866.

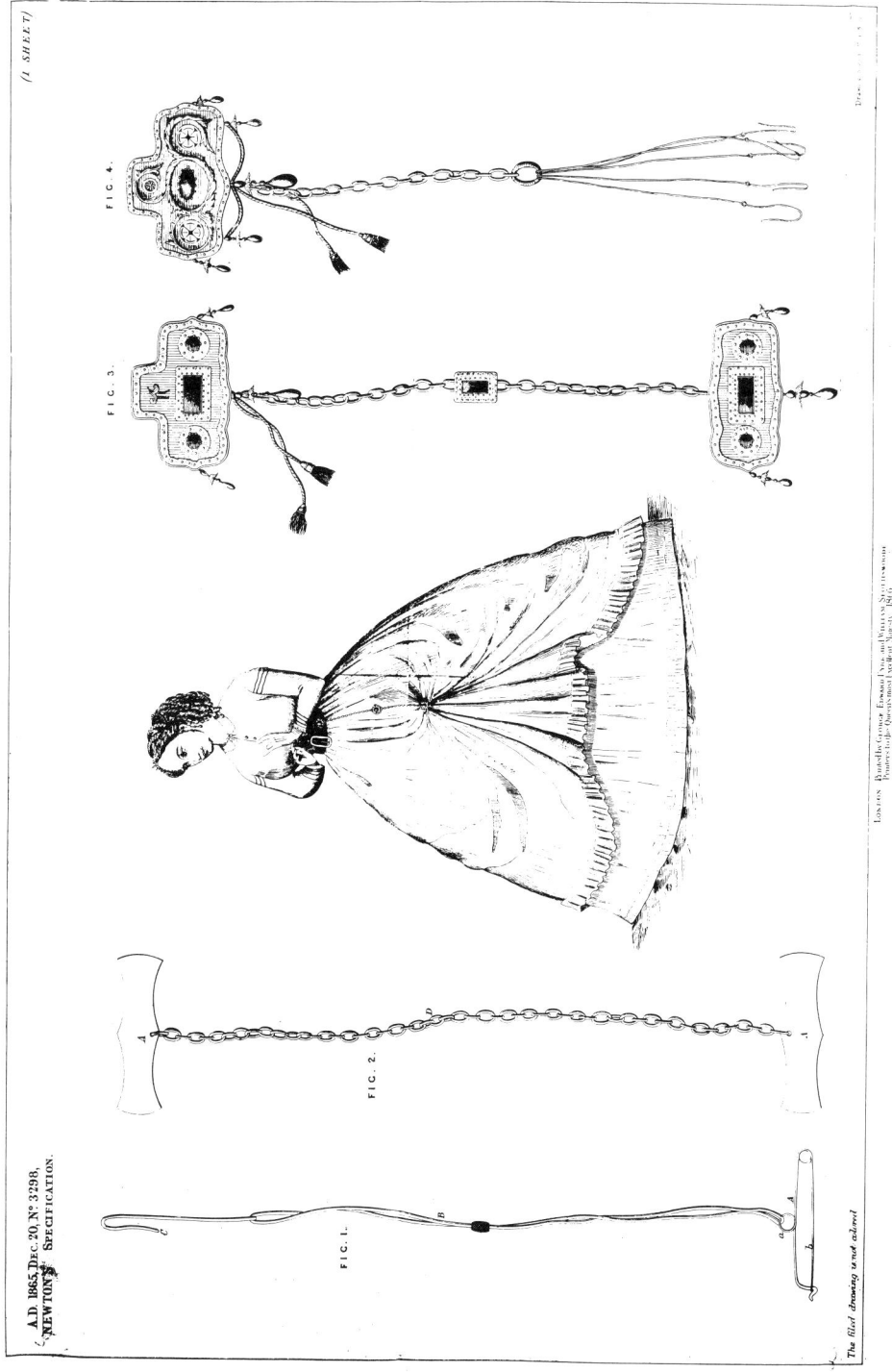

There were many descriptions and names given to the new inventions to be used for this quick and easy method of raising the skirt. As we have seen, the original term was porte-jupe or porte-robe, but in the book *Abridgment Class Wearing Apparel*, the words skirt or dress suspender-holder or fastener were used. For example, in 1865, H. E. Newton's Patent 3298 for the 'Improved Dress Holder' describes a device for holding up ladies' dresses to prevent them from trailing on the ground consisting of a brooch, which is attached to a chain or cord to a second brooch or to a hook secured in a belt. Any number of brooches, but preferably two, may be fastened round the belt.

> All the arrangements that have been proposed hitherto for holding up ladies' dresses and preventing them from trailing in the mud or dust have more or less attained the desired result.
>
> The arrangements which have hitherto been employed (one of which consists of a nipper, between the jaws of which the material is retained) have been found very inconvenient, inasmuch as after a certain time the jaws of the nipper become bent, and the dress will slip away therefrom and fall on the ground. This system has given place to an arrangement of cords which will loop up the dress, and will partially effect the desired object, but at the same time with detriment to the elegance of the dress.
>
> The object of the present Invention is to attain all the desired results, and it consists in the employment of brooches, either straight or bent, arranged vertically or horizontally, and intended...to unite in one or many points the several folds of the dress.
>
> In some cases, where the material employed is likely to be injured by the pin of the brooch small rings can be placed at proper intervals round the dress. The lower brooch may be dispensed with, and small chains with hooks may be used instead, as shown in Fig. 4. In Figs. 3 and 4 the brooches are represented in an ornamental form, but this is not absolutely necessary. Fig. 5 represents the application of this system and the effect produced. It will be understood that by raising the cord or chain to which the brooches or fasteners are attached, and supporting it from the girdle, the dress will be looped up and prevented from trailing on the ground.

According to Bethnal Green Museum, safety pins, as we now know them, were not patented until 1876. What is called a 'modified safety pin' is used in H. E. Newton's 'Improved Dress Holder' (Illustration 4) as is shown in Fig. 1 at A. This consisted of a small box, called a 'brooch', covering the point of the pin. Nevertheless, the pins of these brooches sometimes tore the material and so Newton devised hooks to be used with rings. Remember, no safety pins were available for the baby's nappy – perhaps they used the pin like the one in Fig. 1 rather than the 'brooch' type.

From the 1860s, many women's magazines detail all sorts of different skirt grips and lifters. For example, the *Young Ladies' Journal* of 1 July 1868 carries a description of the latest lifter:

> A new porte-jupe is called The MacAdam. It is a sort of brooch looping up the skirt on either side.

Moreover, the walking costume and the full-dress toilet required different handling, as the latter was more dignified with its ample skirt and sweeping train. The time-consuming ways and the trouble taken to dress as elegantly as possible occupied much magazine space. Here, the descriptions were combined with recommendations as to the most suitable way for keeping the hem of the

5   *Drawn from Memory* by E. H. Shephard 1957

skirt clean. Current costume historians of Victorian and Edwardian days are well aware of the different numbers of underskirts and petticoats and top skirts that were worn then. When dressed in these, with or without a crinoline, it became necessary to have some control in their handling.

Indeed, contemporary sources indicate the care taken to raise the skirt without showing too much ankle or petticoat. Fashion proclaimed, at certain

6 *Drawn from Memory* by E. H. Shephard 1957

periods, that a coloured petticoat was pleasant enough to show, providing the dress were lifted just to the right height. No washing machines were available, of course, and, as materials were not cheap, dresses were made to last some considerable time. In these circumstances, caring for your dress was important, especially for the middle class – in contrast to women farm workers, who wore no petticoats, often washed their dresses and skirts and wore no dress suspenders.

However, many of the middle-class ladies who did not have the use of a carriage, had not learned or been taught the elegant skill of raising the train of their skirt over their arm. In fact, no mention is found of the use of skirt grips in the etiquette books of that time. To quote from *Antiques from the Victorian Home* by Bea How it is suggested that:

> Skirts fitting close round a lady's hips then flaring out into a wide beruffled hem that trailed along the ground – a skirt if not upheld by a dainty gloved hand encountered many dangers. So a skirt clip was invented to help ladies from having continually to hitch up their skirts when crossing a street or to avoid getting them wet on meeting a puddle. These little objects took the form of a lucky horse-shoe or a fan, a shell or a brass butterfly. It has been said, though, that a skirt clip, however pretty, would *not* have been used by 'carriage' ladies or

7   Marie Tempest 1900

by a lady of the upper class world. She would have disdained them, preferring to bend down gracefully and pick up her skirt with one hand.

The late Alan Mansfield, co-author with P. Cunnington of *English Costume for Sports and Outdoor Recreation*, was convinced that the very ornamental skirt grips were 'rather non-u and used by the lower classes risen-up'. Anne Buck, author of *Victorian Costume*, supports this view, as in a letter she wrote to me:

> Expert elegant management of the skirt was a social skill, which can be noted in contemporary fashionable scenes.

The charmingly written autobiography of E. H. Shepard (1879–1976), which was also illustrated by him, includes his childhood memories of his aunts and

8   *Cassell's Family Magazine* 1879

recalls how they dressed. For example, Aunt Fanny has her skirt duly girded (Illustration 5) and her skirt 'hitched up' while she is waving at the train on a summer's day (Illustration 6).

The photograph of Marie Tempest, taken in 1900 (Illustration 7), shows her skirt lifter in the form of a hand, probably made from wood. It also shows her

9   *Cassell's Family Magazine* 1879

lifter strung around her neck or possibly attached to her chest with ribbons. Thus her hands were free enough to enable her to hold the chain of the dog. This seemed a convenient way of dealing with long skirt trains and is also to be seen in *Cassell's Family Magazine* in 1879 (Illustrations 8 and 9). However, perhaps the most attractive skirt grips were used by ladies in the ballroom. These were made of gold with a gold or pinchbeck chain to join up with the skirt clip. The skirt clip itself may have been in the shape of a shell with enamel decoration. Silver was also used.

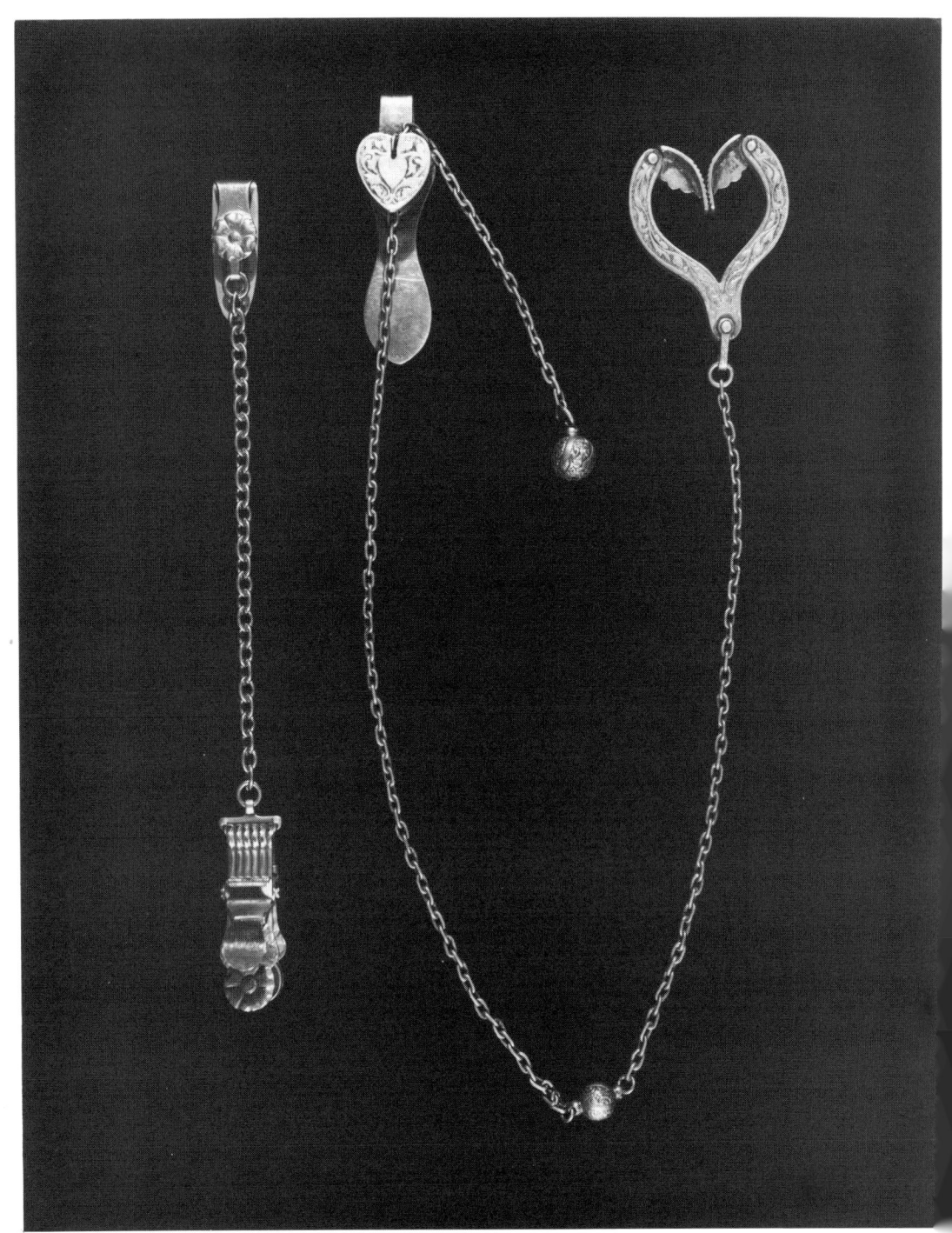

10 The 'Grappler' grip, *Glenbow Museum, Calgary*

In 1903 the 'Grappler' was advertised by N. C. Reading & Co., and it was made of 'Albo' silver. Reading & Co. were jewellers as is indicated in Kelly's Directory for Birmingham. The photograph from the Glenbow Museum, Calgary, Canada, of the 'Grappler' grip has a different chatelaine clip from those found in this country. The hip clip obviously matches the grip, but the design is slightly different from the one shown. The inscription on the hip clip reads 'The Grappler Adjustable Dress Holder NRC'.

An average customer would find it difficult to describe a special grip when looking for one in a shop. They did have descriptive names, however, as can be seen from this incomplete list, which were somewhat crude and often in French:

Acme	The Fob
The Alexandria	Fyfe's A.B.C.
The Alston	The Graham Patent
The Automatic	The Grappler
The Automatic Eadie's Patent	Imperial
Beau Ideal	L'Imperitive
Bicycle	Invincible
Bijou	The MacAdam
Blackwood's Magic skirt elevator	The Patent Victor
Breese's Bee	The Perfait
Brevette	The Queen
The 'Chic' Dress Raiser	The Rink
The Clifton	Le Securite
The Clinker	The Shakespear
The Crown	Simplex
Depose	The Superior
Duples	Surprise
Eclipse	The Times
Esigrip	Trianon
Eureka	Unwanti
The Firm	

Sometimes the appearance of the grips was enhanced by decorative chains. This enabled the wearer to feel at ease should they show. Indeed, the more decorative the chain, the more likely it would have been for the grip to be displayed. The use of black or brown cords was very common and they were lighter to wear than a chain and less visible. The cords were of dark silk, which covered the jute and were worn round the waist. If, instead of wearing a belt or a skirt, a one-piece dress was worn, this rendered a hip clip and chain useless, hence the cord. It can be understood from the worn-out condition of many cords that they were used frequently. Moreover, some grips were used so often that the

11 Badminton player c. 1880 'Battledore and Shuttlecock' *The Graphic* 1871 (Wimbledon Lawn Tennis Museum)

silver plate was worn away, allowing the brass to show through. This also indicates the exact method of fingering.

Some grips had large rings formed by the levers when they were locked and holding the skirt. This large ring was big enough to enable a fan, an umbrella or a parasol to be set inside it, so serving two useful purposes. The hand was then free to use the fan or parasol, whichever was not held in the clip that was lifting the skirt.

The cost of grips varied, of course, and they seemed to be obtainable from many different haberdashers. For example, the 'Rink' dress suspender sold for 3/6d in 1876; it was described in C. Cunnington's book, *English Women's Clothing in the Nineteenth Century*, as follows:

> A dress-holder hooking on to the waist and from which two chains six inches long are suspended at the end of which various forms of clips are fastened to hold up a portion of the skirt.

The 'Stella' chain dress-holder advertised in the *Army and Navy Catalogue* of 1902 cost 1/6d. The 'Security Cycling Dress Holder' cost 6d per pair from Harrods in 1909. The 'Automatic' was advertised at one shilling in the *Young Ladies' Journal* of 1891, and the 'Chic' was only 1/4d for a double set. The gold dress-holders are now sometimes to be bought from jewellers, so we may assume that this is where they were first obtained.

To wear long and full skirts when playing games presented some difficulty. Illustration 11 shows the back view of a woman playing badminton. Here, a ribbon lifts the skirt to some extent, but a skirt suspender has also been used at the centre back. We can only guess how the ladies playing tennis managed their skirts! Great care and trouble had to be taken to allow enough room for leg movement during a game while ensuring the skirt was only lifted to a decorous height (Illustration 12). Predictably, *Punch* took an interest in such fashionable niceties; Illustration 13, the cartoon of the tennis player garlanded with the cord of a skirt grip, appeared in 1879 – the tennis belle had taken considerable care of her long train. *Punch* published the following article in March 1860:

> In the window of a dressmaker's shop in Bond Street there is a comical picture giving three views of a fine lady, in the elegant and simple costume of the period, exhibiting the use and application of an invention named 'L'Imperatrice' by reason that it is said to be worn by the Empress of the French, otherwise and in the vulgar tongue called a Dress-Holder. It has the appearance of a small rake – the handle of which is held, or hooks on to the waist; the teeth, or whatever answers their purpose, being hitched in the skirts. Next to making dresses of a convenient length, this is perhaps the most commodious contrivance for keeping them up out of the dirt. If, however, appearance were consulted without regard to a little additional expense, the office of the Dress-Holder might be more splendidly accomplished by means of a small winch or windlass attached to a

12 Lawn tennis c. 1880

girdle or waist-ribbon, and carrying a silk line with a weight and a hook at the end of it, by means whereof the dress might be hoisted up or let down at pleasure. The winch being made of gold jewelled with a variety of precious stones, and the hook and weight also composed of the most valuable of the metals, would render the contrivance ornamental in some degree higher perhaps than that of its utility. Moreover, a proper addition would be made to the present very moderate cost of ladies' dresses, which is much too closely accom-

A HISTORY OF VICTORIAN SKIRT GRIPS 27

13 'Lawn-Tennis Costume', *Punch* 1879

modated to the meanness of husbands and fathers. If one winch would not suffice, two might be employed; and the process of winding and unwinding them would constitute a new study for those who delight in giving their mind to the observation of feminine actions.

Less condescendingly, the *Housewife* of 1895 featured popular dresses (Illustration 14). Here we can see that there was a loop half-way down the skirt so that the hand was able to lift the skirt and therefore a metal grip was not required. Fortunately a few advertisements still exist in which dress holders are

14 The *Housewife* 1895

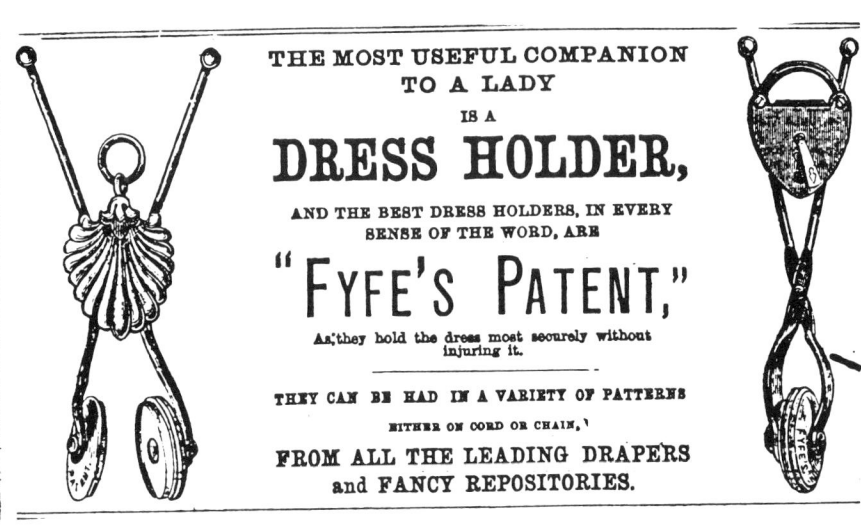

15 'Fyfe's Patent', the *Queen* 1878

IZOD'S PATENT CORSETS

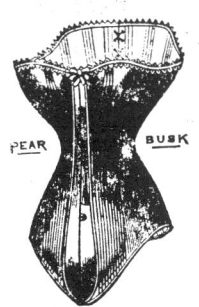

These Corsets may be had of all respectable Drapers and Ladies' Outfitters, at various prices, and in a variety of material—viz., White, Dove, and Grey Coutille, Single or Double; White and Dove Satteen, also in Scarlet Lasting, and Black Italian Cloths.

They are made with either Plain or Pear-Shaped Busks.

The Belted Corset is also produced.

Only such Corsets as bear our Trade Mark Stamped on them are Genuine and Warranted.

Upon the shape of the Corset entirely depends the accurate fit of a Lady's Dress or Costume. The Patent Corsets of Messrs. Izod & Son are cut in exquisite proportions, made of the best materials, and finished by their Patent Steam-moulding Process, so that the fabric and bones are adapted with marvellous accuracy to every curve and undulation of the finest type of figure. These Corsets also give great support, and they fit so accurately and comfortably that a very small size can be worn without the slightest injury to the figure.

The variations in fashion are vigilantly watched, and every necessary alteration is made to adapt these Corsets to the prevailing style of dress.

The quality of the materials used, and the accuracy in fit of each Corset, are maintained through every change of fashion.

The Patentees desire to call special attention to their Trade Mark.

"The Steam-moulded Corsets of Messrs. Izod & Son have obtained a justly-merited place in public estimation. These Corsets are composed of the best materials, are cut in exquisite proportions, are finished by steam-moulding, and are acknowledged model types of female form. Thus manufactured, it is by no means surprising that the feminine portion of the public inquire for these admirable Corsets of Draper and Milliner, and that the demand for these Corsets is increasing daily."—*The Milliner and Dressmaker.*

"Lay figures or models have been constructed in exact accordance with Hogarth's Line of Beauty. Ample space is secured for the play of the chest and lungs, thus at the same time preserving health and proving the contour of the figure of the wearer."—*The Queen.*

Any Corsets not bearing this Trade Mark are not genuine, and only imitations.

FYFE'S PATENT DRESS-HOLDERS

The only ones which were awarded a Prize Medal at the recent Paris Exhibition.

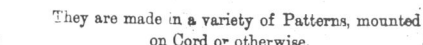

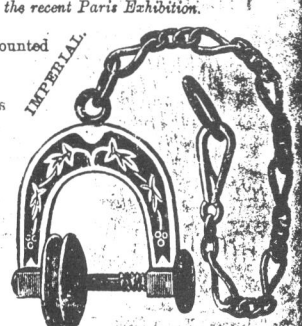

They are made in a variety of Patterns, mounted on Cord or otherwise.

To avoid purchasing Imitations, Ladies should see that the name, "FYFE'S PATENT," is stamped on the Holder.

They can be had from all the leading Drapers and Fancy Repositories in the United Kingdom.

DR. J. COLLIS BROWNE'S CHLORODYNE,
THE ORIGINAL AND ONLY GENUINE.

If you wish a quiet, refreshing sleep, provide yourself with that marvellous remedy—viz., CHLORODYNE.

CHLORODYNE is the best remedy for Coughs, Consumption, Bronchitis, Asthma, Diphtheria, Fever, Croup, Ague, Diarrhœa. It is the only specific in Cholera and Dysentery; it cuts short all attacks of Epilepsy, Hysteria, Palpitation, and Spasms, and is the best palliative in Neuralgia, Rheumatism, Gout, Cancer, Toothache, &c.

BEWARE OF PIRACY AND IMITATIONS.

Sold in Bottles at 1s. 1½d., 2s. 9d., 4s. 6d. None is genuine without the words, "Dr. J. Collis Browne's Chlorodyne," on the Government Stamp. Overwhelming Medical Testimony accompanies each bottle. Sole Manufacturer,

J. T. DAVENPORT, 83, Great Russell Street, Bloomsbury, London.

16 'Fyfe's Patent', *Journal du Grand Monde* 1879

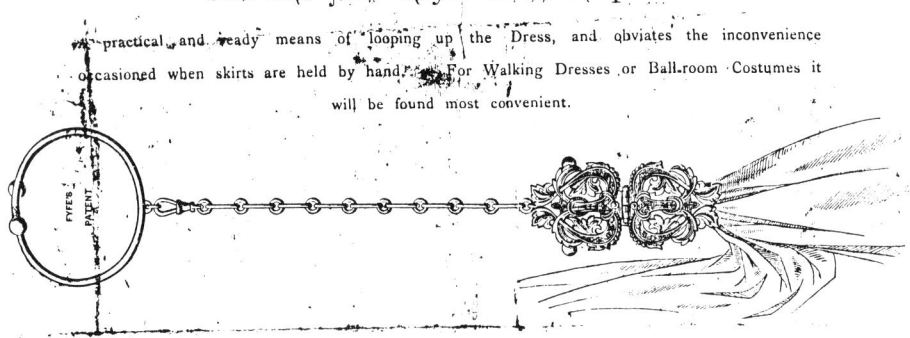

17   Fyfe's patent for the 'New Royal Dress Loop'.

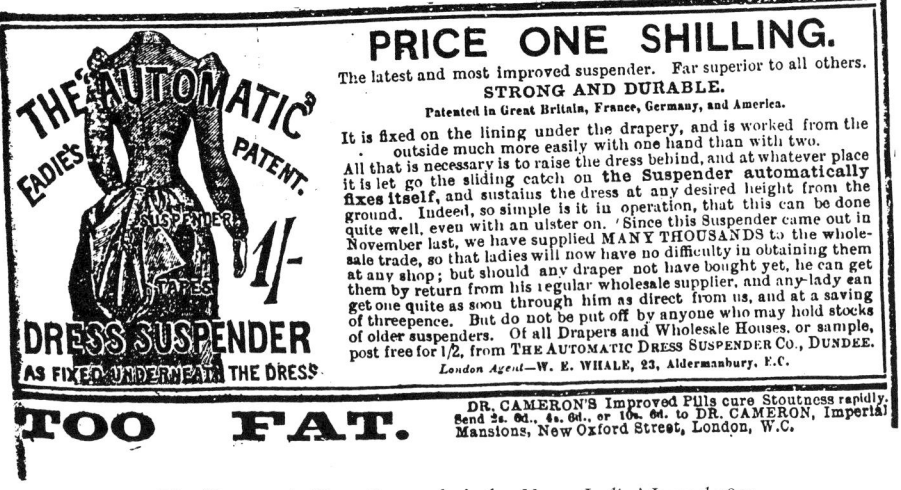

18   The 'Automatic Dress Suspender', the *Young Ladies' Journal* 1891

illustrated and described (Illustrations 15, 16). For example, Fyfe's became one of the best known firms and they duly advertised their goods. The above advertisements appeared in the *Queen* in 1878 and the *Journal du Grand Monde* in 1879. Where the Fyfe advertisement originally appeared is unknown, but it may have arrived with the 'New Royal Dress Loop' when, it was first sold. The advertisements for the 'Royal Dress Loop' are now to be found in the Victoria and Albert Museum (Illustration 17).

DRESS SUSPENDER.

As the trains even of outdoor dresses get longer and longer, a serviceable dress holder becomes more and more indispensable. Many devices and arrangements have been tried, but none of them with unchallenged success. What we expect of a dress suspender is to grasp the dress tightly, and to retain its hold firmly without injuring the material in any way; besides, the mechanism should be capable of being easily applied, as well as of being easily detached. Of all the dress holders which have come under our notice, the one constructed by Messrs Thornhill, of 144, New Bond-street, of

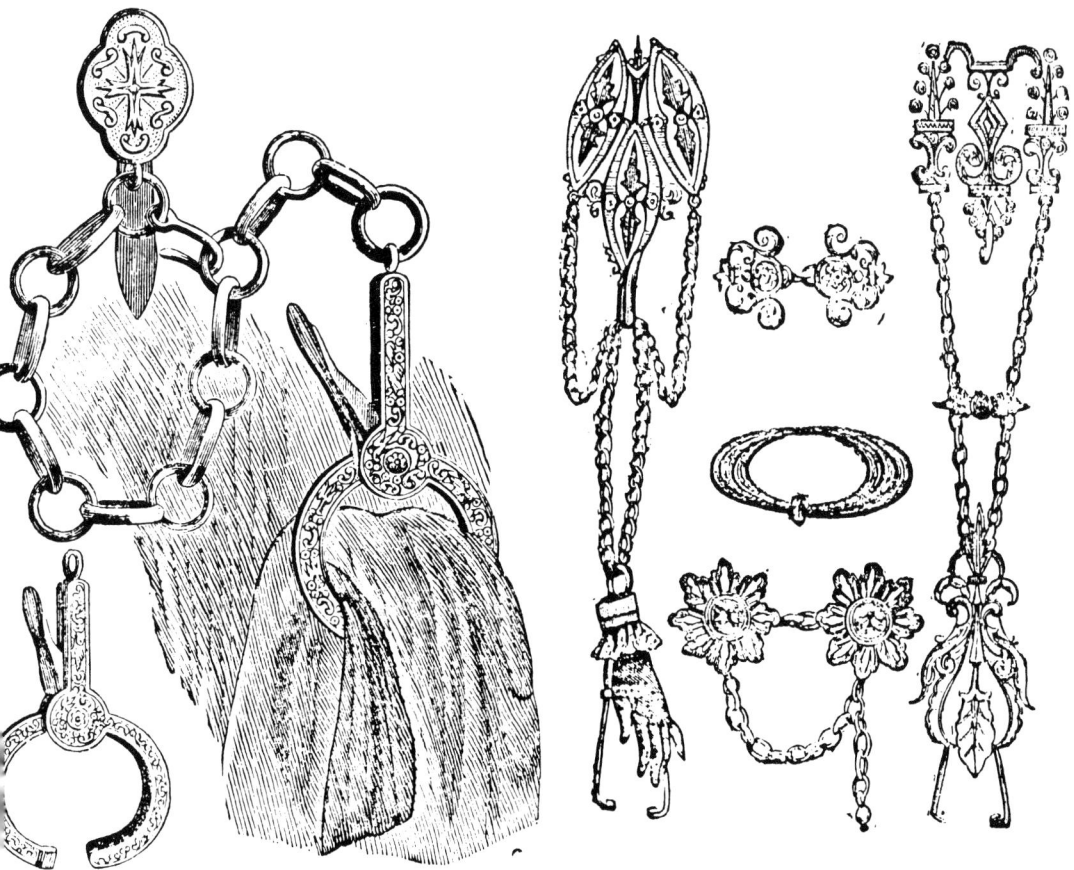

which we give an illustration, answers each of these requirements best. The movable arm of a cut ring pushes the folds of the dress between two prongs, and holds them there by the pressure of three rounded knobs, fitting into each other; the catch is easily attained by pressing the two halves of the ring together with the hand, and a touch on the projecting lever detaches the dress immediately. Any injury to the material between the smooth surfaces of the silver prongs is impossible, unless the former be mere gauze. Cloth and silk will bear the unavoidable strain of this dress holder perfectly well

19 'Dress Suspender', the *Queen* 1876

It is also worth noting that the 'Automatic Dress Suspender' advertised in 1891 was said to be the latest and most improved. It was, we read, to be fixed underneath the dress, emphasising that dress suspenders were not meant to be seen – always! The makers of the 'Automatic' were the Automatic Dress Suspender Co., Dundee. It was patented in Great Britain, France, Germany and America, according to the advertisement in the *Young Ladies' Journal* of 1891 (Illustration 18).

It is an old saying that if a craftsman wants his work to last, he should avoid using materials which are precious in themselves – in particular gold and silver embellishments which could be melted down and used for other purposes. Despite this, the metal used for skirt grips were described in the *Queen* in 1870 as including:

> Different metal, such as gold, bright frosted and oxidised silver, nickel and steel with engraved, pierced chased and relief surface to suit the different styles of dress.

Indeed, the dress suspender made by Messrs Thornhill of 144 New Bond Street (Illustration 19) is described as having 'the smooth surfaces of silver prongs'. The illustration in the *Queen* on 22 April 1876, gives a rare glimpse of another new silver dress holder (Illustration 20).

On the other hand, grips made for everyday use were usually of second-rate metal, such as plated brass or white steel. These were worn on most occasions – even when fishing the skirt grip, apparently, made trousers unnecessary!

On the actual dress holders themselves was often stamped the maker's name and the date of the patent or design registration number – or both. As a decorative feature, the name or initials of the owner might be moulded on the lock. Were these bespoke orders? When they were obtainable from the haberdashery counter at the local shops, there were obviously many designs from which to choose. If interested in birds, then the peacock, parrot or the heron appealed; if the woman's husband or another relation were in the Navy, then an anchor was appropriate. Do we assume, therefore, the husband of the owner of the pig decoration (see plates 1–6) was a farmer? The grips with horizontal screws were of brass and strongly made. They appear to have been suitable for holding a riding habit with the lady riding side-saddle. Flowers as decorations were popular and butterflies were often included as a lock.

In 1890, the 'Chic Dress Raiser' was patented, and it was advertised in the *Ladies' Journal* 1 December **1891**. The ladies presumably understood how the use of the 'Chic' would make their skirts rise to the right level. They had to use their own skill in stitching the dress raiser to their dress. An advertisement states that the 'Chic Dress Raiser', 'Recommended by Madame Abelina Patti', is used by royalty. Queen Victoria was a great walker in the Highlands, so maybe she was the royalty to whom the advertisement referred.

20 'Fashionable Toilettes', the *Queen* 1876

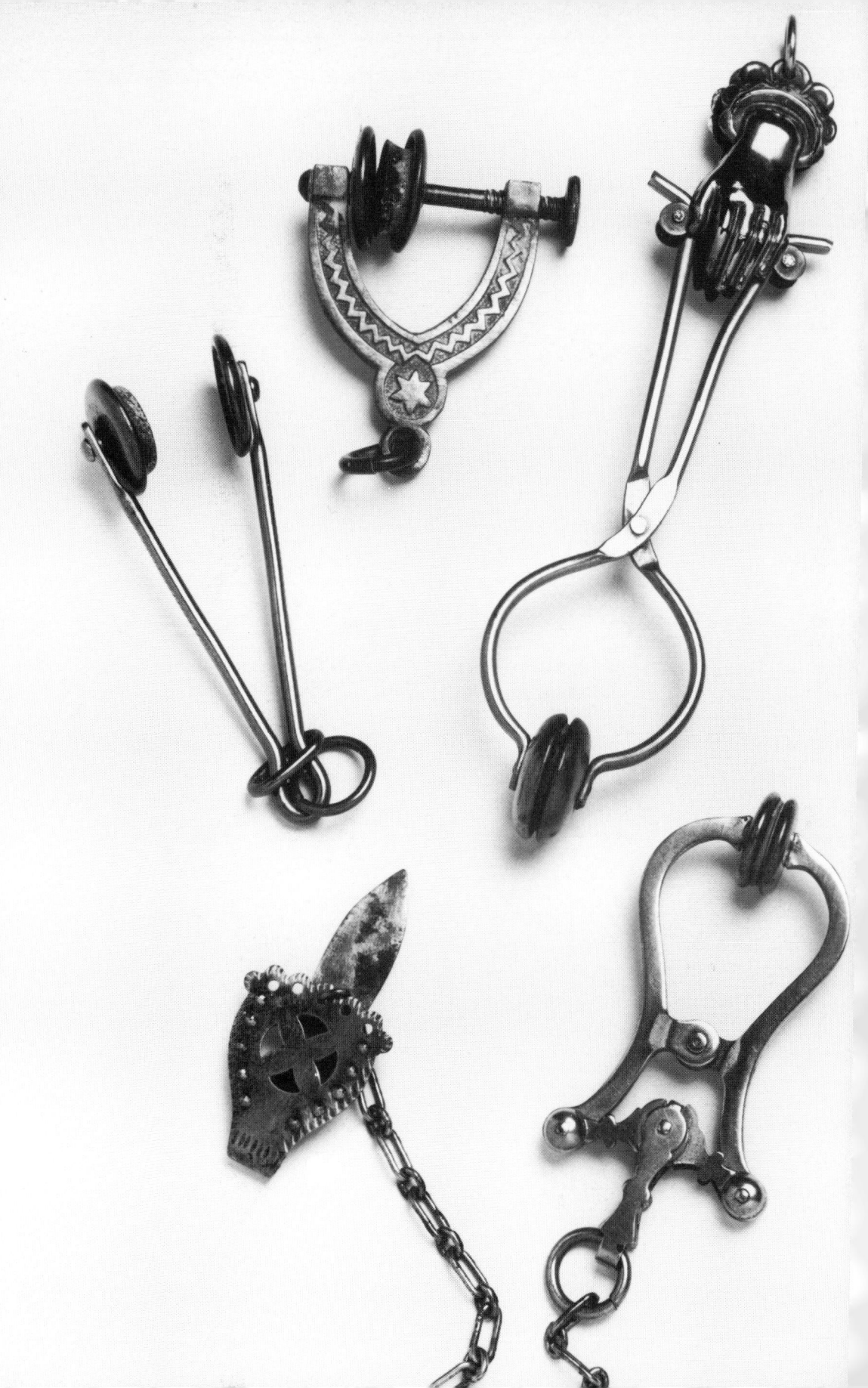

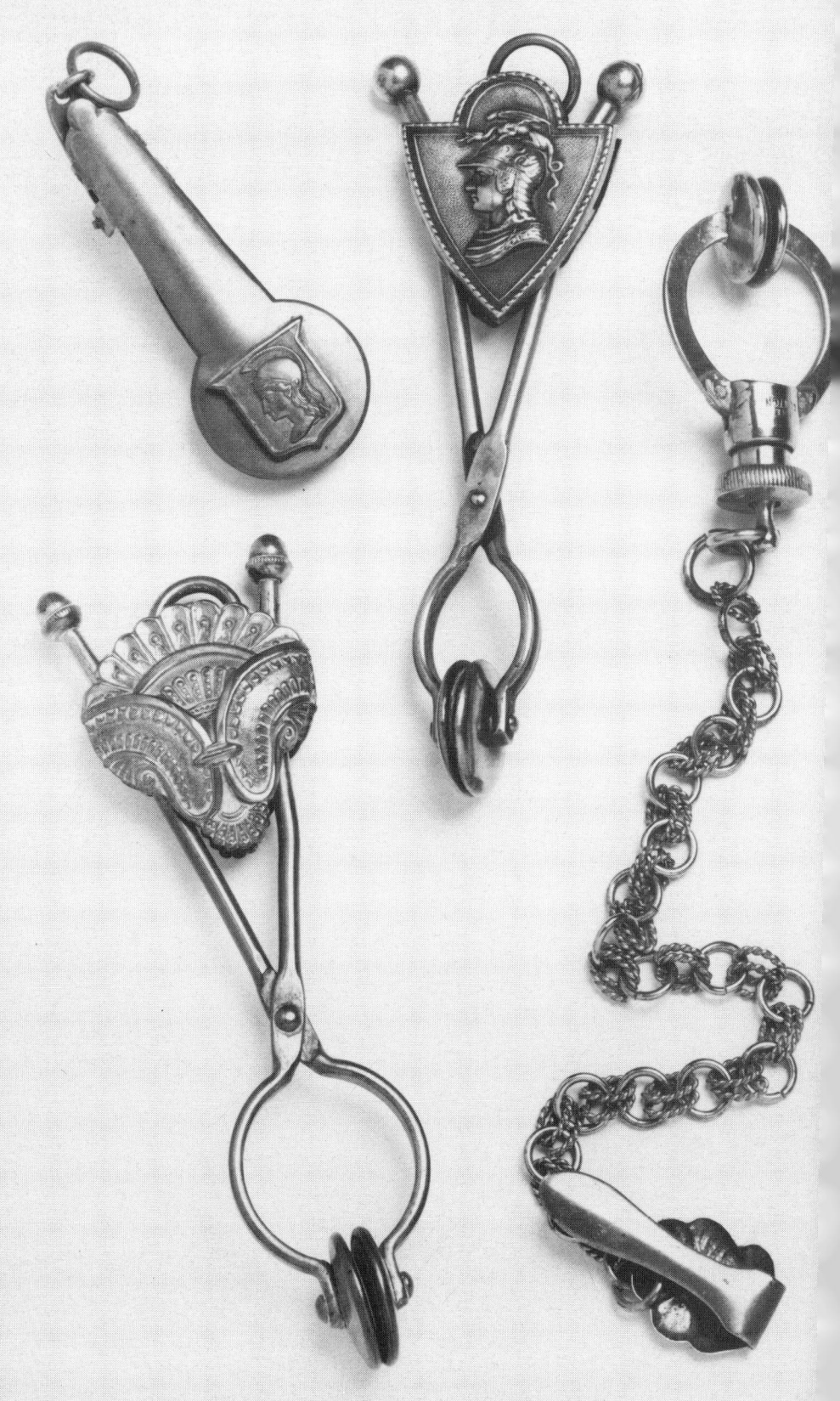

21 'Damassé Silk and Satin Evening Toilette', *Harpers Bazar* 1881

The lady who is obviously taking much care dressing herself, and is also being assisted by her maid is advertising the silk and satin toilette of 1881 in *Harpers Bazar*. She carried her grip, which is attached to her fan. It is one of the simplest brass grips, but is it her fan or her grip which is attached to her wrist and was her skirt grip similar to the one pictured?

22   Skirt lifter 1876

The American-manufactured 'Blackwood Magic Skirt Elevator' was used inside the skirt from 1876 (Illustration 22). The dotted lines indicate that it was not seen and it was also possible to change it from one dress to another. An alternative way of looping the train appears in the *Queen* in 1878. A silk cord was passed through rings that were sewn on the skirt so that a demi-train could be looped up to look like a short skirt.

Although most dress fastener manufacturers worked in London, Birmingham or Paris, the inventor Elijah Stanley came from Walsall, Stafford. His Patent 4478, entitled 'A New or Improved Lever Fastener For Holding Ladies' Dresses and other Articles', states that:

> this article can be made with any metal or wood, or bone or ivory, or vulcanite, or made of any metal and covered with leather or fabric of any description.

The firm Olney, Amsden and Sons (Illustration 23), who advertised the 'Fob' dress holder, worked in London from 1874 to 1884. However, the 'Fob' may have been imported as the firm was listed as being a wholesale haberdashers, foreign importer and trimming warehouseman. The original advertisement for the 'Fob' dress holder, dated 1890, is at Abington Museum, Northampton.

23 The 'Fob' dress holder c. 1890 (Abington Museum, Northampton)

A HISTORY OF VICTORIAN SKIRT GRIPS

The Germans also made grips to support skirts as late as 1904. (Illustration 24). Dress clips were sometimes worn in pairs: the 'Alston Dress Suspender' (Illustration 25) demonstrates this use, as does the pair at the York Museum.

The various changes in the methods employed to keep skirts off the ground prompted a lively correspondence in the women's magazines of the 1870s. In a letter to the *Queen* in January 1876, a woman called Lottie wrote:

> I would therefore recommend the old plan of loops and buttons on the skirt under the tunic – I had a dress made for me last month arranged in this way and it answers admirably. There are in all seven buttons sewn on a few inches below the waistband. The distance of the loops from the buttons will, of course, depend on the height of the wearer.

von Orth and Duisberg's Improved Suspender for Skirts and the like allows the garment to be lifted to any desired height, gripped in place firmly, and then let down again at the wearer's will.

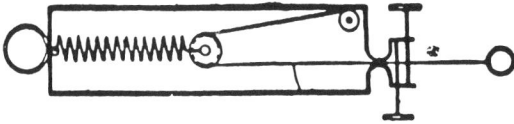

11106/1902
Dr Ludwig von Orth *Engineer*
9 Ludwigkirchstrasse, Berlin, Germany

Martin Duisberg *Manufacturer*
133 Koepenickerstrasse, Berlin, Germany

(Herbert Haddan & Co)

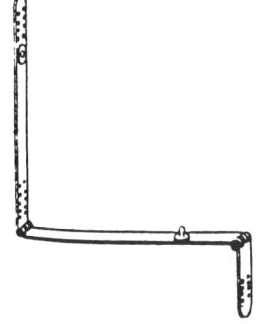

Brune's Device for lifting Ladies' Skirts comprises three hinged bars sewn to the skirt and is specifically designed so as not to cause creases in the material.

1174/1904
Paul Brune *General Agent*
19 Friesenplatz, Cöln, Germany

(Ferdinand Nusch)

24   Von Orth and Dursberg's 'Improved Suspender for Skirts and the like' 1902; 'Brune's Device for lifting Ladies' Skirts' 1904

Similarly in the *Queen*, 26 February 1876, there is a description of a complicated way of looping the skirt that appears after the directions on the use of tapes and ways of tightening the skirt over the petticoat. Again, later in the same year, a woman called Nellie wrote in to ask if:

> Anyone who has used the new chatelaine dress holder could inform me whether it answers the purpose, also where I can get it – are directions given for using it?

Arden Holt replied on 13 May:

> Chatelaine Dress Holder – These new dress holders answer perfectly where the skirts are so arranged, that the front and side breadths are of comfortable length, the back only very long. They may be bought at Bedlake, Burlington Arcade; or indeed almost anywhere; there is very little to learn about using them. They hook on to the dress at the side of the waist; the side attached to the ball prongs is slipped, so that they open easily.

In February yet another solution had been put forward for the continuous trouble of keeping the skirt out of the road:

> A good and easy plan is to put a casing across the back breadths as far as the side seam and put in it two tapes, one at each end, to come out in a hole (button holed over) in the centre. You put the casing about half a yard from the waist, or whatever depth suits. You can draw the strings a little to keep back the skirt, and when walking draw it as much as is necessary to keep the fronts tight over the petticoat, and tie them around the waist, it is such a simple plan and so quickly arranged.

Other accessories include attractive and decorative metal clasps with two chains which attach them to the chatelaine. There are no padded discs on these accessories, and their original use is unclear. Were they glorified skirt lifters or were they clasps to be used for holding a fan or a purse or the dance programme? It is not clear what the teeth would actually grasp but it is doubtful that they were used for lifting the skirt because they might have torn the material. Discs used in the original skirt lifters were nearly always padded.

It will be noted that skirt lifters used for long Victorian skirts did not appear to have been patented until 1876, though various methods for hitching up the skirt before that date were patented. The latest date of a patented skirt grip registered in this country seems to be 1892, and the German ones were patented in 1904. Many interesting descriptions of the inventions made during Victoria's reign can be found in the Public Record Office, and this may involve a trip down into the vaults to find Victorian Patents. Some patents have illustrations and show that there seem to have been as many grips patented as there were wearers. It is possible to tell from the records which manufacturers produced the most favoured of these accessories. When advertising became more acknowledged, the names and products of the better known manufacturers

XLIII.—The "Alston Dress Suspender" is an article that will command much appreciation among all classes of the feminine community. It combines the advantages of both simplicity and security and its lightness and portability render its use applicable on any and every occasion when the wearer wishes to raise her dress from the ground without the necessity of carrying it. For golfing, walking, or touring, it will be found of invaluable service. It is readily adjusted to any height, and claims to be the only dress suspender which places ladies' skirts in perfect safety. Yet another thing to be urged in favour of the "Alston Dress Suspender" is the fact that it will not injure the finest of dress materials. This unique and withal simple suspender is but a length of fine chain, with larger rings set at regular intervals. The extremity of the two chains that descend the dress are furnished with strong safety-pins, that are pinned through the skirt. The chain traverses the waist-belt or band at the back of the skirt for the space of about five inches, where it is furnished with two flat hooks that slip securely over the band. These hooks are also furnished with small exterior hooks, over which the intersecting rings of the chains are passed to regulate the length of the dress. Both the band and ring-hooks, or clips, are smooth and flat, thus occupying no material space in waist measurement. The "Alston Dress Suspender" can be carried in the palm of the hand, or a watch pocket, without incumbrance, and be adjusted in a few seconds to the band of the dress or belt, or it can be worn attached and be left loose until it is found necessary to loop up the skirt by the safety-pins. A special advantage in this suspender is the fact that the weight of skirt suspended from it is graduated across the back of the figure and does not depend from one point, which is the not infrequent cause of great discomfort and weariness to the wearer.

25 The 'Alston Dress Suspender', the *Housewife* 1895

became more widely recognised. On the whole, the less successful manufacturers' names appear less frequently in the Patent Book.

In some cases the registration numbers or Patent numbers indicated on the items cannot be found at the Public Record Office. This may be because, as it

26a Skirt-lifter, late 19th. century. White metal clasp, and hook with classical head. (York Castle Museum)
26b Fyfe's patent 'Surprise' skirt-lifter, late 19th. century. With decorative white metal cover for the clasp. (York castle Museum)
26c Skirt-lifter, 1870–1880. White metal with long black cord. (York Castle Museum)

A HISTORY OF VICTORIAN SKIRT GRIPS

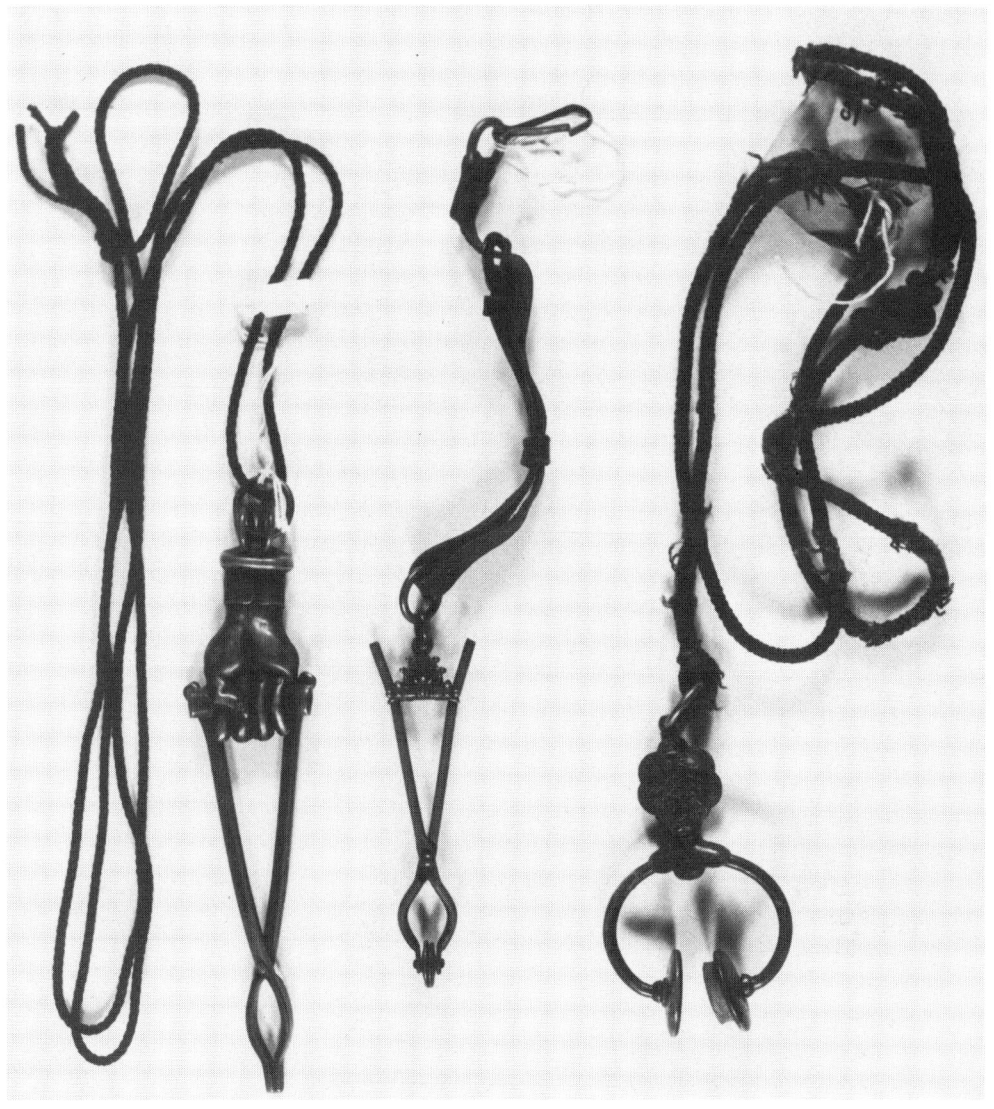

27a Skirt-lifter, 1876–1880. Gold-coloured metal with long black cord. Stamped 'Regd. Novr. 14 1876.' (York Castle Museum)
27b Skirt-lifter, 1870–1880. Gold-coloured metal with short leather strap. (York Castle Museum)
27c Fyfe's patent 'ABC' skirt-lifter, 1876–1880. Gold-coloured metal with long black cord. Stamped 'Registered Sept. 21 1876.' (York Castle Museum)

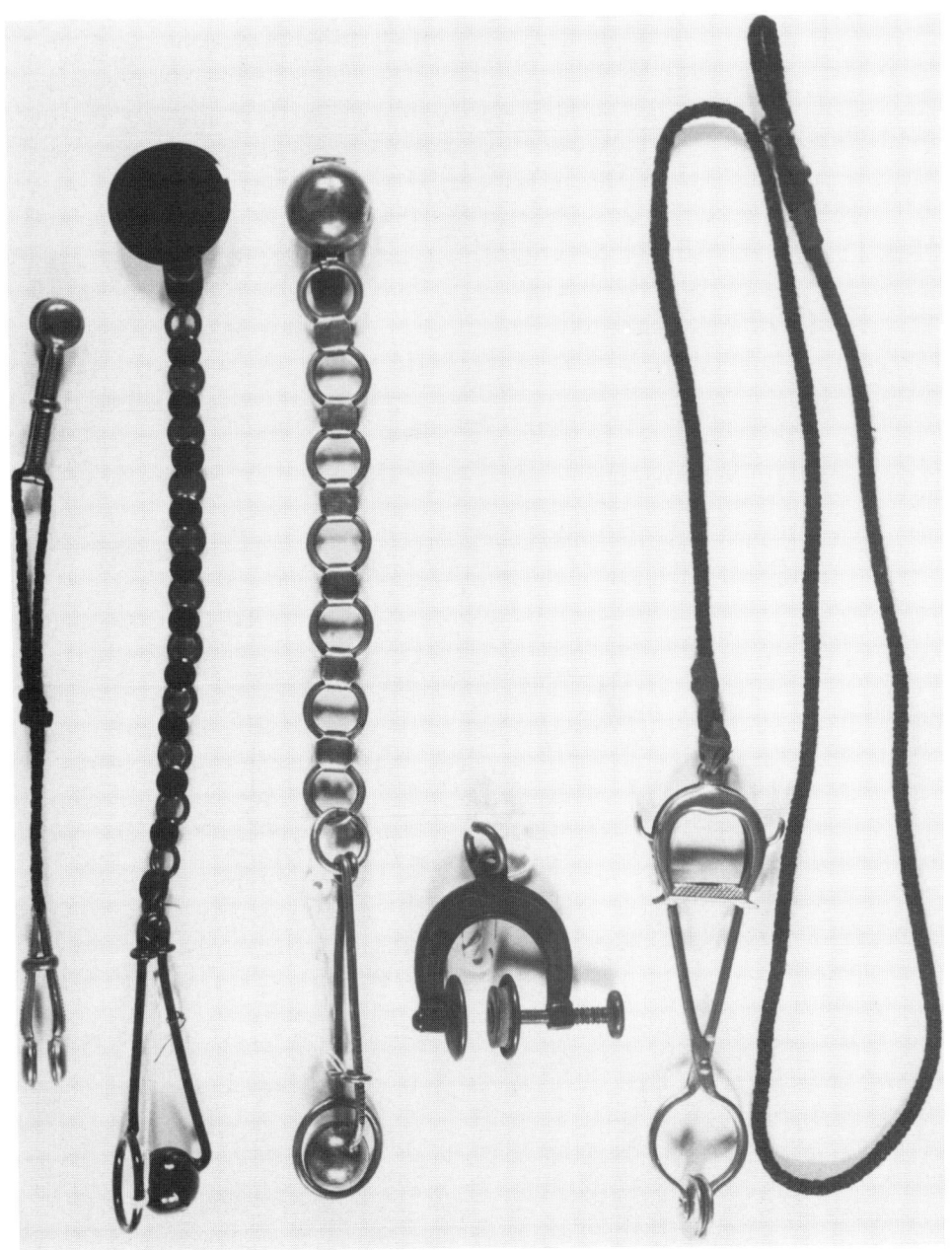

28a Skirt-lifter, late 19th. century. White metal and short black cord. (York Castle Museum)
28b Skirt-lifter, 1870–1875. Chain ornamented with discs of French jet, clasp black painted metal. (York Castle Museum)
28c Skirt-lifter, 1870–1875. White metal. (York Castle Museum)
28d Horseshoe-shaped skirt-lifter, gold-coloured metal, stamped 'Fyfe's ABC patent registered Sept. 2nd. 1876.' (York Castle Museum)
28e Skirt-lifter, white metal, late 19th. century. With long black cord. (York Castle Museum)

cost money to register a patent, it was cheaper to put a fictitious number on the item to deter copiers. The number on the article could, of course, refer to something totally different.

Skirt clips were still used between the two World Wars. They were used when cycling to school, adjusting skirts that were – by that time – not too long. An elastic cord or belt went round the waist, and the actual grip may well have belonged to mother from before the First World War. Then, of course, skirts became even shorter, and the need for skirt grips faded away.

A.D. 1876, 23rd June. N° 2593.

Dress Suspenders.

LETTERS PATENT to Alexander Leslie Fyfe, of Aldersgate Street, in the City of London, for the Invention of "IMPROVEMENTS IN LADIES' DRESS SUSPENDERS."

Sealed the 1st September 1876, and dated the 23rd June 1876.

PROVISIONAL SPECIFICATION left by the said Alexander Leslie Fyfe at the Office of the Commissioners of Patents on the 23rd June 1876.

ALEXANDER LESLIE FYFE, of Aldersgate Street, in the City of London. "IMPROVEMENTS IN LADIES' DRESS SUSPENDERS."

5 My Invention relates to an improved construction of lady's dress suspender by which the dress is more securely held than by these articles as at present made.

According to my Invention the suspender, which is attached to a chain provided with a hook for attachment to the waistband, consists of a spring clip of peculiar construction by which the dress is held. This clip consists of a pair of jaws
10 spoon shaped, cupped or hollowed, and having the one a spring pad or cushion, which fits in the hollow of the other and thus securely retains the dress. The said pad or cushion consists of a disk of metal, cupped or hollowed, with a spiral spring behind it, and is fitted in the hollow of one of the jaws, as above mentioned. The jaws are provided with a runner so formed as to embrace and compress them
15 firmly together at the point where the dress is held. The runner may be of any desired form, and the back of the jaws may be corrugated or roughened transversely to ornament them, and at same time retain the runner more securely in position.

SPECIFICATION in pursuance of the conditions of the Letters Patent filed by the said Alexander Leslie Fyfe in the Great Seal Patent Office on the 19th
20 December 1876.

ALEXANDER LESLIE FYFE, of Aldersgate Street, in the City of London. "IMPROVEMENTS IN LADIES' DRESS SUSPENDERS."

My Invention relates to an improved construction of ladies' dress suspender by which the dress is more securely held than by these articles as at present made.

25 According to my Invention the suspender, which is attached to a chain provided with a hook for attachment to the waistband, consists of a spring clip of peculiar construction by which the dress is held. This clip consists of a pair of jaws, cupped

or hollowed, and having the one a spring pad or cushion which fits in the hollow of the other, and thus securely retains the dress. This pad or cushion may be made of india-rubber, velvet, cork wood, or other suitable material. It, however, consists preferably of a disc of metal, cupped or hollowed, with a spiral spring behind it, and is fitted in the hollow of one of the jaws, as above mentioned. The jaws are provided with a runner so formed as to embrace and compress them firmly together at the point where the dress is held. The runner may be of any desired form, and the back of the jaws may be corrugated or roughened transversely to ornament them, and at same time retain the runner more securely in position.

Description of Drawings.

Figure 1 shows a front view of my improved clip or suspender. Figure 2 a vertical section through the spring jaws, showing the same in the open position, and Figure 3 a similar view of the jaws as closed to hold the dress.

A, B, are the two jaws of circular, oval, or other suitable form in face view. These jaws are attached to a wire spring shank C, which is coiled into a loop at D, serving to attach it to a chain and to impart the necessary elasticity of the shank to make the jaws A, B, spring open when released. Each jaw A, B, is made of thin metal stamped up in the cupped or hollowed form shown, and the jaw B has fixed in it a spring pad or cushion E, also made of thin metal cupped or hollowed, as shown, and held in place by the spiral spring F behind it, which is attached at one end to the jaw B and at the other to the pad E. This pad is received in the hollow of the jaw B, as shown, and serves, when the jaws are closed on the dress, to press the latter into the hollow of the jaw A so as to hold the dress securely, but with an elastic pressure to avoid injury to the dress. The surface of the pad E may be corrugated or roughened to assist in holding the dress. G is a runner sliding on the shank C, and formed so as to embrace the jaws A, B, as shown, and press them firmly together when slid down to the position shown in Figure 3, the jaws being thus compressed directly opposite to the point where the dress is held. The runner is made of metal, and may consist of a body part G slotted to slide on the shank C and formed in one piece with two rigid jaws G^1, G^1, which embrace the back of the spring jaws A, B, as shown. The latter may have their outer surface corrugated transversely, as shown in Figure 1, to prevent the jaws G^1, G^1, accidentally slipping off.

Having described the nature of my said Invention, and the manner of performing the same, I declare that what I claim as the the Invention to be protected by the herein-before in part recited Letters Patent is, a ladies' dress suspender, consisting of a pair of cupped jaws A, B, provided with an internal pad or cushion, the jaws being attached to a spring shank, and pressed together by a runner embracing the backs of the jaws, substantially as shown and described.

In witness whereof, I, the said Alexander Leslie Fyfe, have hereunto set my hand and seal, this Eighteenth day of December, in the year of our Lord One thousand eight hundred and seventy-six.

A. L. FYFE. (L.S.)

LONDON: Printed by GEORGE EDWARD EYRE and WILLIAM SPOTTISWOODE,
Printers to the Queen's most Excellent Majesty. 1876.

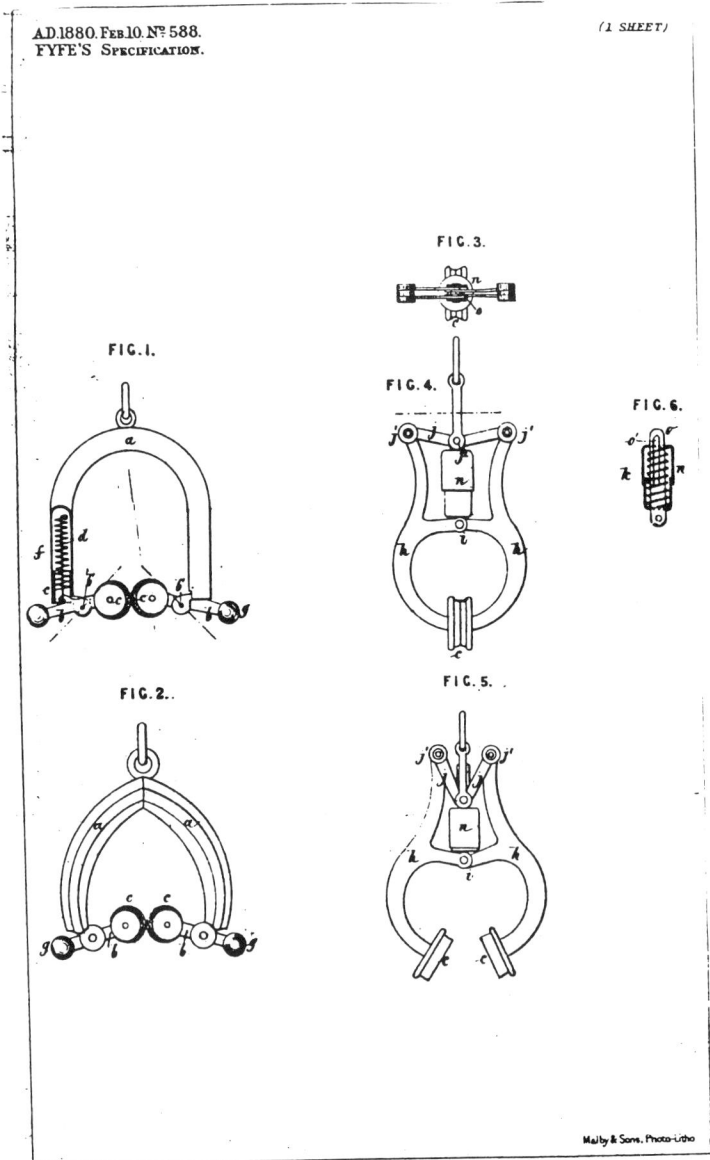

A HISTORY OF VICTORIAN SKIRT GRIPS

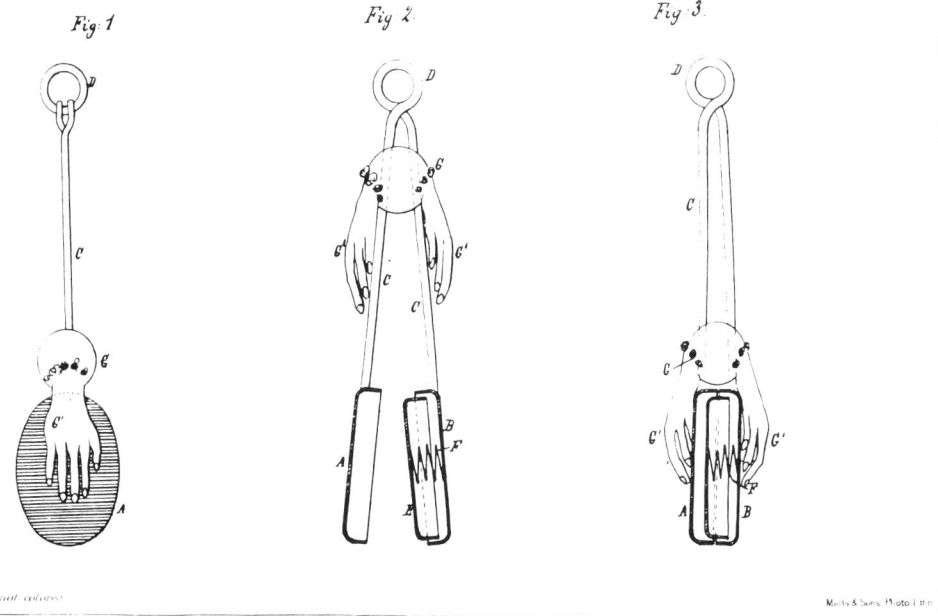

A.D. 1876. June 23. N° 2593.
FYFE'S SPECIFICATION.

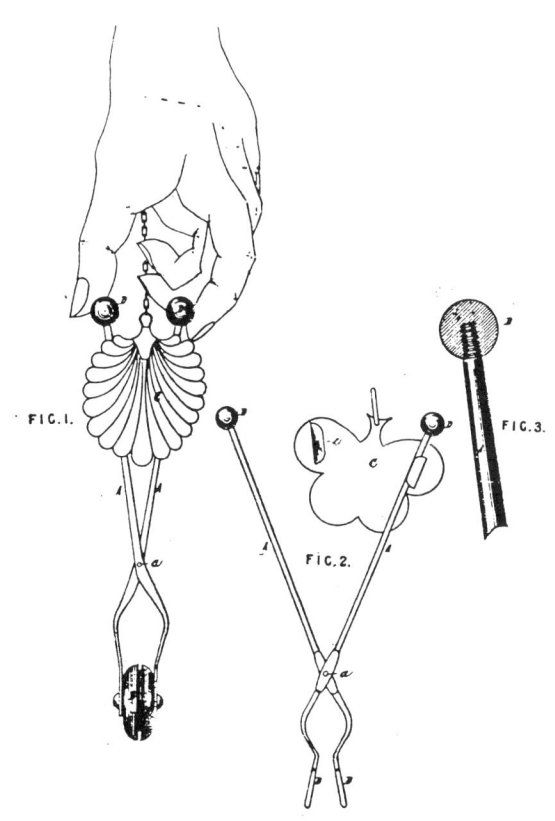

A.D. 1878, 5th November. N° 4478.

Dress Fastener.

LETTERS PATENT to Elijah Stanley, of Walsall, in the County of Stafford. Manufacturer, for the Invention of "A NEW OR IMPROVED LEVER FASTENER FOR HOLDING LADIES' DRESSES AND OTHER ARTICLES."

Sealed the 2nd May 1879, and dated the 5th November 1878.

PROVISIONAL SPECIFICATION left by the said Elijah Stanley at the Office of the Commissioners of Patents on the 5th November 1878.

ELIJAH STANLEY, of Walsall, in the County of Stafford, Manufacturer. "A NEW OR IMPROVED LEVER FASTENER FOR HOLDING LADIES' DRESSES AND OTHER ARTICLES."

The principle involved and operating in this article is that of "resistance by pressure." In the simplest forms of the article the following is the "*modus operandi.*"

The dress or other garment, twill, or fabric, intended to be secured is placed through a ring adjusted on a plain or ornamental body, which is suspended by a cord or strap to the waist or shoulders of person wearing the same, or hung from the dress or other article by means of safety pin, clasp, or other similar device, or depending from any fixed or elevated point, and which body is so arranged that the portion of fabric inserted through ring shall, in the act of releasing itself, draw towards itself, and put into operation the lower part of the body, causing the mutual approach of body and ring, and exerting a pressure upon the inserted part of fabric which effectually prevents its escape.

Other forms of the article are triangular, oval, square, &c., of such designs as rustic, Oxford cross, anchor pattern, or crescent, or to effect the greater security in particular fabrics, or to make assurance doubly sure the approach of two parts of holder is compelled by a spring, or the two parts alluded to are uniform and worked or stamped to produce the relative and respective features enumerated, but in all cases the principle operating and relied on is the same as explained with relation to simplest form as above.

Stanley's Improved Dress Fastener.

The advantages of this Invention are numerous. Other holders are complex, and consist of many parts; this simple, consisting essentially of but one or two at most, except where spring is required, or in case of an elaborate design.

Facility is another of its advantages.

The adjustment of dress is easily effected, and when desired, as easily released; it is only required to lift the ring or put the body in a horizontal position to withdraw the fabric instantly.

Security.—The fabric cannot escape however light or heavy its weight, and where the strain is great the hold is great, and not as in most descriptions of dressholders where the reverse is the case.

Lastly. The fabric is not injured by the operation of the holder. No tong or sharp sides to cut or narrow aperture to tear and crease, and as the pressure is always proportional to the strain, the full power of holder is only rarely exerted, giving the advantage of slight grasp in ordinary use, a powerful grip in case of strain, but a firm hold always.

Another advantage is that this article can be made with any metal or wood, or bone, or ivory, or vulcanite, or made of any metal and covered with leather or fabric of any description.

FIG.1.

FIG.2.

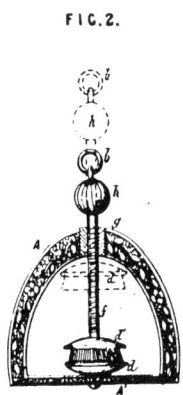

FIG.3.

Stanley's Improved Dress Fastener.

SPECIFICATION in pursuance of the conditions of the Letters Patent filed by the said Elijah Stanley in the Great Seal Patent Office on the 3rd May 1879.

ELIJAH STANLEY, of Walsall, in the County of Stafford, Manufacturer. "A NEW OR IMPROVED LEVER FASTENER FOR HOLDING LADIES' DRESSES AND OTHER ARTICLES."

The principle I adopt in this Invention being resistance by frictional pressure, increasing in power as the resistance becomes greater, and in accomplishing this object I make use of the well known principle of the lever in the following method:—I make a frame of any suitable form, and by a cord, chain, hook or in any other way suspend the same by its narrow end; on this frame I hang a ring, not necessarily round, in such a way that the upper part of the ring shall be on one side of the frame, but at its greatest diameter it shall be on the other side of the frame, and at its lowest point the ring shall be just below the lower edge of the frame. The frame and ring are set to such a form that the lowest part of the frame fits into the ring, and when not in use, lies inside it. In use the dress or material is drawn up into the ring, and under the lower part of the frame, and is then allowed to hang down. The weight of the dress would cause it to withdraw itself from the ring, but the friction of that part of the material which is through the ring acts by its friction upon the lower part of the frame, thereby causing the aperture to become smaller, and causing the grip of the frame and ring to become intensified. In some forms of this Invention I propose to insert a spring, fixed or otherwise, to act in such a way upon the upper edge of the ring as to always keep it in contact with the frame at the upper part of the ring; this spring must be sufficiently flexible to allow the ring to open from the frame at least to a right angle.

In the Drawings annexed Figure 1 represents the dress-holder as it would be suspended, but not in use, A being the frame; B, the cord by which it is attached to the waist; C is the ring; and D, the spring attached to the frame at E pressing upon the ring C at F. Figure 2 represents the dress-holder open previous to the insertion of the dress, and Figure 3 shews the dress-holder with the dress G drawn through it.

The same letters indicate the respective parts of the Invention in each Figure.

Having now described the several parts of my Invention, I wish it to be distinctly understood that I do not limit myself to the form or figure as shewn in the Drawings, as the Invention can be modified as fashion dictates, but I claim as my Invention a dress-holder acting by frictional pressure increased by leverage.

In witness whereof, I, the said Elijah Stanley, have hereunto set my hand and seal, this Twenty sixth day of April, One thousand eight hundred and seventynine.

ELIJAH STANLEY. (L.S.)

WILLIAM MASON,
    Witness to the signature of
    Elijah Stanley.

A HISTORY OF VICTORIAN SKIRT GRIPS

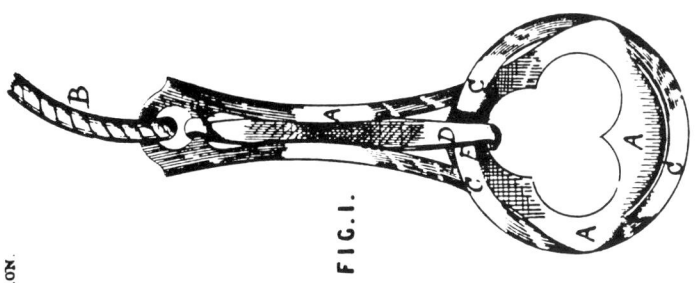

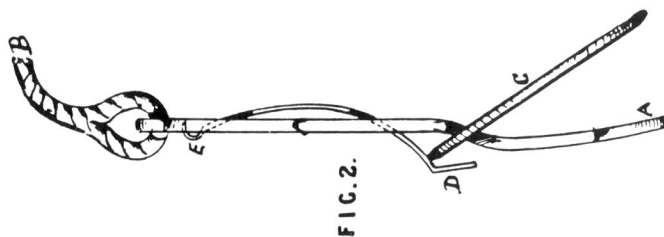

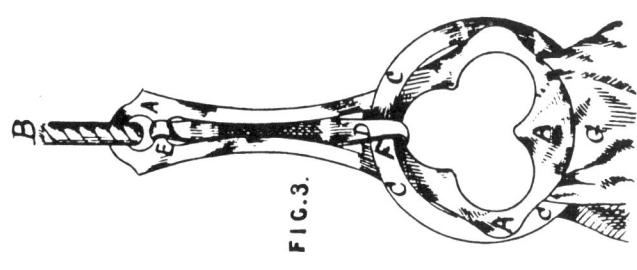